G

FEB   2007

MARGRET & H.A.REY'S
Curious George
at the Parade

Illustrated in the style of H. A. Rey by Vipah Interactive

Houghton Mifflin Company   Boston

Based on the character of Curious George®, created by Margret and H. A. Rey.
Illustrated by Vipah Interactive, Wellesley, Massachusetts: C. Becker, D. Fakkel, M. Jensen,
S. SanGiacomo, C. Yu.

The text of this book is set in 17-pt. Adobe Garamond.
The illustrations are watercolor and charcoal pencil, reproduced in full color.

Library of Congress Cataloging-in-Publication Data

Curious George at the parade / illustrated in the style of H. A. Rey by Vipah Interactive.
p.   cm.
Based on the original character by Margret and H. A. Rey.
Summary: George's curiosity creates chaos at a holiday parade.
RNF ISBN 0-395-97833-5 PAP ISBN 0-395-97837-8 PABRD ISBN 0-395-97845-9
[1. Monkeys — Fiction. 2. Parades — Fiction.] I. Rey, Margret. II. Rey, H. A. (Hans
Augusto), 1898 – 1977. III. Vipah Interactive. IV. Title: Margret and H. A. Rey's Curious
George at the parade. V. Title: Curious George at the parade.
PZ7.C921355   1999
[E]—dc21   99-21454
                                                              CIP

Manufactured in the United States of America
WOZ 10 9 8 7 6 5

This is George.

He was a good little monkey and always very curious.

Today George and his friend, the man with the yellow hat, were in the city for the big holiday parade.

They found a place in the crowd, but an announcement had just been made.

"The parade may not start for a while, George," the man said. "The wind is too strong for the big balloons. Let's go in this department store while we wait."

George and his friend looked around the store as they waited for the wind to settle down. Suddenly, something strange caught George's eye. What could it be? He was curious.

But when George looked out the window,

6

he didn't see anything strange. He saw the parade! He saw floats, clowns, and jugglers, and a band standing in straight rows.
Then George thought he saw an elephant eating a treat.

That made George hungry.
(It had been a long time since
breakfast.) Now he could think
only of finding a snack.

Why, here was a treat just
like what he ate in the jungle:
fresh nuts—right off the tree!

George was lucky to be a
monkey...

he simply climbed out the window
and jumped into the tree!

Then he pulled and pulled. But
the nuts would not come off the
tree. They were not so fresh after all.
In fact, they were not even real. But
George did not know that.

He pulled harder and harder. The
tree began to sway...

Suddenly, there was a loud SNAP!

Then, CRASH!
Down came the tree.
Down came George.
And down came all the nuts!

Luckily, George was not hurt. But still he did not have a snack.
He raced after the nuts. He chased them around the elephant and
under the clown, then in and out of the band's straight rows. "My
perfect rows!" the bandleader cried. "You've ruined my perfect rows!"

13

The bandleader raced after George. He chased him down the street and around the corner, but he was not quick enough.

Where was George?

Soon the bandleader tired of searching and went back to straighten his rows. He did not know where the little monkey had gone — George was nowhere to be found.

George was not sure where he had gone either — and the nuts were nowhere to be found. After all that, George had lost his snack. After all that, George had lost his way. Now how would he get back to the department store and back to the man with the yellow hat?

Just then a bus was stopping at the corner. George liked to ride the bus. Maybe it could take him back to his friend. Quickly, he hopped on the bus and away they went.

From his seat up on top,
George could see everything.
The bus rounded a corner.
Here was something familiar!

But something was wrong. Two balloons had drifted off course—
their ropes were tangled. The parade helpers were trying to fix them
and a crowd gathered to watch. As the bus came to a stop, someone

yelled, "Catch that monkey! He's ruined our parade!" It was the bandleader, and he was pointing right at George! George did not want to be caught, but there was no way for him to get down. There was only one way to go...

George grabbed a rope and went UP!

Up, up he climbed, higher and higher. He was a little frightened, but he held on tight. Then he heard someone call: "GEORGE!" It was the man with the yellow hat! George was happy to find his friend. The man was happy, too.

George swung from one rope to another. Now he felt like he was in the jungle swinging from vine to vine.

"Look," someone shouted from below. "The little monkey is fixing the balloons!"

Then George swung safely into the arms of the man with the yellow hat! The crowd below cheered—the ropes were no longer tangled!

When George and his friend arrived back on the sidewalk, it was time to start the parade.

The bandleader was no longer angry—George was a hero! Even
the mayor came to meet George. "I hear you created quite a stir,
George," he said. "But at last everything is in order. Would you like
to ride with me in the parade?"

Soon the balloons started moving, the music started playing, and the band marched down the street in straight rows.

And there, leading the whole parade, was Curious George.